funkhaus

T0154874

funkhaus

hinemoana baker

Victoria University of Wellington Press

Victoria University of Wellington Press
PO Box 600 Wellington
New Zealand
vup.wgtn.ac.nz

Copyright © Hinemoana Baker 2020
First published 2020

This book is copyright. Apart from any fair dealing
for the purpose of private study, research, criticism or review,
as permitted under the Copyright Act, no part may be reproduced
by any process without the permission of the publishers.
The moral rights of the author have been asserted.

A catalogue record is available at the National Library of New Zealand

ISBN 9781776563142

Printed in China by 1010 Printing International

for Mum

. . . avant-garde poets hate poems for remaining poems instead of becoming bombs; and nostalgists hate poems for failing to do what they wrongly claim poetry once did.

—Ben Lerner, *The Hatred of Poetry*

If we begin here, none of us will make it to the end
                              Of the poem.
Someone has to make it out alive, sang a grandfather to his grandson,
His granddaughter, as he blew his most powerful song into the hearts
    of the children.

—Joy Harjo, 'How to Write a Poem in a Time of War'

CONTENTS

MOTHER

Mother is a north wind and she stops the trembling.
Mother has hands of flax and butter.
Linseed and two-stroke, all the same
we hear the rain try and squall.

Mother is Ūkaipō and East Coast.
She is not north this early morning.
Feet of cause and effect, feet of bridges.
All of the mother around us, all of the mother
under and above us: with her we feel un-clumsy and on-shore.

The adzed and hand-smoothened
mother of play, of katakata, of laugh.
Mother of church and kindergarten, of live and die.
Mother of born. She calls me dreamer, knee-kicker, nail-biter
calls me in to eat. My feet are a plant, in real life too.
Whakataka te hau, kia hii ake ana te atakura.

Mother oh Mother, now no one can make
a non-human object out of me! Mother
oh Mother, we have half a bright red hour
we have the whole bled-out night through.

If you have to be diving, Mother, be deep under
with a good heavy roof of ocean on you, good engineering.
Mother of Language and Mother of Land.
Flaxfuls of seed and a hand in your hand.

IF I HAD TO SING

I have no idea what to call this rebirth
and yet I'm here to name it
to feed the new flame

with wood from the old.
Language is a flute, a lily,
a chair overbalancing,

a church we teeter
on the threshold of.
There are places where

they harvest water from the air –
drink fog from a glass then overnight
hang the rag back on the bayonet.

Does a thing which is reborn
need to have died?
All those cities still live

in my mirrors, they rise
and fall again with the sun's
rounds, the way the planet

carves its own seismic
trench in the solar system.
The spring charges

and recharges its river system
while on the columns of our lives
press unimaginable stresses.

Hold me up now, as I do you.
Sing, and steady me under
your strong, sure feet.

FLOHMARKT

A woman carries in her arms
a heavy rectangle of sky –
roofs and treetops.
She places it in the back seat
of her car to calm down.

You and I sit
like separate circles
of a Venn diagram
unaware of the fabled
tasting zones of the human tongue.

Unaware that they do not exist.
All of the tongue tastes all of what it is given.
In the bright sun a dog and a bike
exchange insults
through their owners.

I live with a surplus
of chairs, mostly empty.
My one, with its smooth

wooden arms and your one
if you were here.
The kind of chair you never want

to get up out of
the kind of chair for which
prepositions were invented.

FOX

I saw it in the snow outside
a Danziger Strasse apartment block,
swish of the M10 tram behind me
grit under my boots:

barely feral, blaze of copper
and gone. The most powerful things
are the ones we simply come across:

the loss of appetite
the dying in your arms of your own child
how the skin is known
as the third kidney.

Climbing into the air outside your door
a tufty plant grows from a cobblestone.
And there –
there is the sandwich board with pictures of fruit

and words you don't understand
which make nothing happen.

BIRD ORDER

My view is rooftops, winter-blue sky
and a chimney. Four birds take turns
landing and lifting from the lip of the roof
swapping places as they go.

One hangs above the other three,
floats a moment, then drifts back down
as another lifts up into its vacated airspace.
But they all look the same to me,

so now I have lost track.
All I know for sure is
they're the same four birds
just in a completely different order.

THE GOOD SHIP

There are things you will learn
in the course of your life and its corrugations
that you would, perhaps, rather not know.
Shirley Temple's hair wasn't really curly.
Babies masturbate in utero.

Health websites exist where gravity
is referred to as 'the ultimate toxin'.
And this perfectly reasonable-seeming man
a dancer whose grace and smile
are matched only by his genuine tan

with whom you are attempting to have a date
by walking through Berlin's first
truly sunny day this month
and it's March and it's also your birthday
and the two of you are discovering Markets –

Flea, Vegan, Vegetable, Furniture –
among spray cans and toppled bottles and brick ruins
whilst disagreeing and agreeing in equal parts
about small and large things
with warm and gentle laughter

and whose hand resting on the small of your back
lightly, just the fingertips,
feels good and right and makes you shiver
in a good way as you walk beside
the impressive, freshly melted river

comfortably silent between wonderings
about the luxury condos
and the black-smoking orange bonfire
the size of two cars that some neon-vested guy

with a can of accelerant
has just lit in the sunshine
so folks from that glitzy hotel
can later stand in line

and complete their final assigned challenge
of the weekend's motivational seminar
by walking over literal hot coals: this man
who is six feet tall with beautiful eyes

that he uses to look
with fond appreciation into yours
now slows his step a little
to explain how science

is definitely pretty much all lies
and aliens in the shape of lizard people
were largely responsible
for seeding planet Earth

with humanoids and later humans
with all of whom, he adds
the aliens are now mightily
disappointed and quite rightly.

AUNTIES

We had a marching aunty and an eyelash-curler aunty, a headscarves one, a lavender talcum powder aunty and a satin running shorts one. We had an aunty who was laid out on the sheepskin rug by that uncle when she was six, and seven and eight. These might be the same aunties. We had an aunty who died on the same day as her own sister and turned into that white horse on the green hill. A drawn-on-eyebrows aunty who said *I don't care how good they are at yodelling they're giving country music a bad name those girls.*

We had an aunty who lifted her still working arm above her head to make it easier for us to take off her top for the wheel-in shower. Then that aunty who hiki'd her great-grand-baby on her hip and we looked up at her, framed against a bright blue Nelson Bays sky. We had an aunty who said *You're sick* and *You make me sick with your disgusting carry-on both of you girls.*

The aunty who said *How dare you can't you see your mother is upset?* The aunty who said *You make me sick with your embarrassing carry-on.* The one with sea-green eyes and pounamu-black moko kauae who wanted to teach us karanga. The aunty who gave her permission. We had an aunty married to that uncle who cursed us, who told us *You should never be allowed around children* and we never, ever were.

The Tākaka aunty. Reason left that aunty and she followed us to the toilet with a mango in her hand and kept talking. She frowned when she smiled, that aunty. She was always *My grandchildren this my grandchildren that.* We had an aunty who said *Don't worry about me I'll just close my eyes and wake up in Paradise.* One of the aunties was actually a nun. One had hands swollen with arthritis and she always stayed young, very young, too young.

This other aunty was a yodeller for real in the mountains with goats way overseas. She never got married and her name started with a K. And that aunty had another aunty who gambled and an aunty with dirt floors. Those were definitely the same aunties. That aunty, oh man, if she ever won the Lotto she would just be winning back her own fuckin money.

Then there's the aunty who watched him shoot himself, even after she herself was already dead, and applauded with her ghost hands, applauded and screamed her karanga tangi, and then we had that aunty who threw a fridge at her own brother, and in the summer she waltzed us round the room with our small feet tiptoe and clammy on top of her high arches, her feet in cork wedge heels.

There was that one-eyed-dog aunty, the pork-and-pūhā aunty, the pinch-of-salt-in-the-porridge aunty, the Prince Tui Teka song aunty, the crawl-on-her-lap aunty, the fifty-bucks-in-a-birthday-card aunty, the fish-n-chips-for-breakfast aunty, the DNA, the DNA, the DNA, the fits-into-the-whakapapa-here-and-also-here aunty, the pale poached eggs aunty, the aunty who plays the piano like a pianola and sings at the same time while you try to watch and memorise every click of her pink fingernails on the black keys because she's gone now but no. No, silly! That one's your mum.

COUSINS

Cousin meets cousin
and it's thunder. They click and
pounce and hiss past on
a school bus. One's a police
check, one rings like glass.

≠

I see you, I see you there in the family
with your mouth, your mouth is closed.
I see you floating down our river
in the guise of a log. I see you
in your office leaning on a shelf

with your eyes sewn shut
then a little to the right of that morning
staring from your own decapitation
into the distance like you'd seen game
on the horizon, like your family is the game.

You understand the collective.
Your body turns towards the heads
towards the faces and mouthparts
of your kin. You come here for water
you think I will offer you water. I crush you

while the dolphins in the harbour laugh.

≠

Dress. Trap. Goat. These are the vowel
sounds which are the black harakeke moving
like an animal in the wind and rain.
Something hovers and leaves.
You wear your huia feathers and the word that

drives you to your knees. Driven onto rocks, adorned.
The cloak is your mouth, your mouth is your face
and the thread decorating it. Soft and pliable.
I bend this book open;
it lands as a pair of wings from a dead weka.

Figs and cherries on the backs of my hands, balancing.
Kneeling to my superiors.
You pull my chin towards you, stroke
my eyebrow with your thumb.
At our throats are always collars

or greenstone or a black tie,
brightness and blue.
This kneeling becomes a marriage.
The handkerchief, the fluke of the tent canvas,
the collars, the moon. The orange of your blanket,

the weightless pain, the shins and the
shield of the sports team.

DECEMBER

December make me forget May.
Walk with me in summer mist under powerlines
where the loud tūī bells out over the valley.
December I dream about you with your harbour
face in your sunshine hands.

Here we go again writing to each other, December.
On the other side of the aisle you lied about your list.
Mine was all porridge and salted fish, yours
was machetes and Christmas ornaments
drilled with holes and filled with salt.

December, in August the Hutt River flooded but
not for long enough. August went clucking off with a bottle.
In September you walked lightly off the ferry into a drift of
    soft night-rain.
In this yellow square of light above Waiteata
I am a dark bird opening and closing its beak.

THE MOUTH OF THE MAN FROM ST LOUIS

Book is child. Is it making good sound?
These could have been your first words to me

since you tend to drop articles with the second drink.
I can no longer use the word 'concentration' so I will use

the word 'steering', so I am still here
still singing greenery into the trees.

Get your thermos of coffee and sandwiches ready
and your library-loving lineage.

≠

I dedicate this poem to the colour of the water
powering over the edge

water the colour of rust and cum
soil foamy with bone.

≠

My favourite snapshot
is the one of the two chubby kids

in the para-pool, grinning and reaching
for each other the year

before its seams gave out.
Nose to nose they begin

kilometres apart
and nose to nose they end.

≠

The hum, the grate, the scrummage.
I dedicate this poem

to the sounds created while
you fail to tell me about any of this.

To the pool ball balanced
on the end of a pool cue

which is balanced on the end
of another pool cue which is balanced

on the blade of a knife
the handle of which is being held

in the mouth
of the man from St Louis.

≠

NARCISSIST ADVICE COLUMN

Pepper blacks the pan so never
Shake it near me, wait
For the flagrant animation
In my bed base
In mountain situations
Sleep swaddled, wake ecstatic

My frantic menus in your mind
I taste of them all
Refuse to refuse me
Waste your time on my errands
Squeeze your lime
On my lemons

Turn up wearing
The whole bird not just the feathers

NARCISSIST ALONE

Whatever position I lie in
Becomes me, I paw me
I bow my own string at a pitch
Sing feverish in my own sweet ear
I wish on myself, frisk myself
Whisking my whites

With my coloureds all sudsy
Wait for me wait for me
Adore me in catechisms
Wade through my patchy fissures
Make parables praise me
Engage all your gears for me

Pour for me
Pour for me

NARCISSIST DIPS A FINGER

Into sprinkles meant for savouries
Then I lick the leftovers, pick off lids and sniff
I lift my head with whistles
Swill a bit, crinkle cut and chilli-lime
Break it down for my backing vocals
I'm gonna bank my bank balance

I'm gonna heist my hands up
Grandstand and handstand
Heels bruise your spruced walls
Bark at your dogs, farm you out
My op-eds inject you
My stop signs forget you

My wood in your box
My grandfather clock

NARCISSIST AT LUNCH

Sunshine rights itself in the crockery
Now I'm in the building
Sinks and the cisterns play tunes
That I wrote in my happening head
Traffic is me, even Sappho is me
Rad snapshots of me

Make the mags wing off shelves
Licence plates are me, pirate flags
Feature me and my inspiring piracy
Leaves on those trees float
Like silk napkins towards me
Even my own fingers

Yes even my fingerprints
Want my autograph

MASSIVE TUNNEL BORER

The two halves drill towards each other
eating through the mountain
excreting cement.
When they meet
the tunnel could be said

to be complete and the machines
bury themselves on that spot
become part of the mountain
it being uneconomic to retrieve them.
Each half is the size of an aircraft.

Each, no doubt, has its trajectory
mapped remotely from above ground.
What appeals most
is not the action of the tunnelling
or even the burial

these topics having been
well-traversed by other machines
but the way they use their food
how they shit out reinforcement
turning the gravel, the mud

the mountain's insides
into a concrete that prevents
the new tunnel's collapse.
Perhaps this is where
we went wrong.

WHEN WE HOVER

when we hover right up beside the canopy
of that tall tree thrashing in the thunderstorm
and the word *golden* waltzes in
and drinks rain from the dip of your collarbone
for fuck's sake like overnight the trees

went greener but too much beauty
obscures beauty and you *are* golden
and green like the tree then just like in the films
the rubbish truck guys in their
orange overalls tango through

we both say *actually more pink*
than orange under these lights
clearly neither of them has any knee pain
at least the u-bahn is a continent of
demanding voice abusive punitive voice

i recite the poem with the fat gold watch
and the cat's clean open mouth
and the next day a cat howls for springtime
in the stairwell so loud I open my door
remembering the Swedish nursery rhyme

it opens on nothing but dust
and the smell of the ghosts of cats
who have pissed and prayed there for decades
the woman who makes dolls
walks past with her five eyes

I am not a building I say
I have no pull-out map is what I meant to say
so we deal with what comes up
yes right there in the passersby
one horse at a time you stepping

out into traffic with your hand
held up strong and me
thanking every fucker for their help

BALKONIA

I imagined him
bleeding into bandages in a hospital
his cape draped over
the visitor's chair, a shape
of pleats, light and dark.

Instead, I read, he
died open-eyed in the arms
of Lake Geneva
and his sad doctor.

I write to you from sunlight
from *Balkonia!*
The city's best-kept secret!
to say the Erdbeere and
the young, dark opal

Basillicum and the trailing
Rosemarin have each
survived the chill night.
The orange thing looks like it won't
live through the day's sun and wind.

In September
I'll eat whatever strawberries
the Eurasian Jays have left me
pack and rush and
catch or miss my flight.

WAIATA TANGI

we turn to each other and turn to each other
in the mother air of what we want.
   —Robert Hass, 'Sunrise'

i

I was caged
with my siblings
large and small

and blanketed
on and off.
Food in dishes came and went.

Sensations in the soles of my feet such as
might be experienced
by a hen or a human.

Heavy footsteps
one set in particular
towards me

and then something uttered,
something round in the mouth.
What have I accomplished?

Nothing.
What have I gifted?
Nothing.

Air and odour
and a slippery
dripping tongue that drops

out of me.
I pounce when I can and
other times I am overcome.

I posture.
I brake hard.
What are we about

in our fur
and on
our stilts?

ii

A streak of blood
sticky with sun
outside the meat-safe.

A week's worth of dishes
that stinks more with each
piece of chalk I eat.

iii

Did you feel that
she says
spelling it out

as if verbs are just things to do
feel, need, work, play.
Several small earthquakes,

a looking away.
The bathroom alone
has a window.

Shadows are purple,
the owl like a close relative.
The new drum of his mouth.

iv

First thing, there is
the jig and squish of
her eye-rubbing knuckle

right up in the socket,
shaking the bed.
Later, the bodyish feel

of the seat and the bend
we're rounding
then the high-heels

brick-stepper clicking
through the vaulted
chamber of the station.

v

No one has done any of this deliberately.
I didn't mean to grow another set of jaws.
She didn't mean to become

so separated
from the light she throws.
Viewed from above

we could be each other's
talismans or touchstones.
Only one third of the vase

of my body
is filled with water today.
Nothing the piano says is worth

hearing. We tune it out
as if it were a preacher
or a pipe knocking or a parade.

vi

I am not dressed for this weather.
The lacerating stone is whaiapu
a word meaning *flint*

with a sound like *sweetheart,*
darling, love, fiancée.
I stoop and sing like a gourd.

WAITANGI DAY

Into my father's house and onto the carpet
in the lounge seven rose petals
are blown by a hot summer wind.

Some are still crimson and some already
lift and float in sepia. But who is it frankly
that writes these days?

≠

In her song 'The Letter'
PJ Harvey uses the image of a pen
as a stand-in for the penis.

'Your beautiful pen,' she sings. 'Take the cap off.'
Oh Language you soccer fan I still long for you
even after everything we've been through.

≠

The way the decision moves into the body.
A bloodstream and a branch
of nerves, slung on a frame.

The body has been eaten into the shape of a map,
an island or a continent particularly around the jaw.
It is recommended the body remain in motion and

flowing with fluids. There's no telling how many people
will look to the body for answers.
Sometimes the answer will be a hair follicle

sometimes a bone-drill.
'Paper' and 'the body' can be like that
one stepping in for the other at the last minute.

≠

The guy who poses with a gun is usually either
holding it cocked at his shoulder, eye to the site
aiming at a target that the viewer cannot see

or he is holding it on his lap while gripping
the antlers of a deer he has recently shot.
The guy who is pictured with his fingers

in the gills of a fish is usually
on a boat at the time, and possibly dangling
from the other hand a bottle of beer

often a green bottle
or another slightly smaller fish.
Sometimes a man is not pictured at all

but instead we see children, a car
a bulldozer, a boat, a screenshot in neon colours of
his favourite quote from the internet.

Occasionally a person is pictured as a very young child in
black and white or even on their own wedding day
with other faces smeared out to avoid we presume

a breach of privacy.
And this is what Waitangi Day is all about
I say to myself and the man on a cliff-edge

pictured cleverly as if he is standing in mid-air.
Waitangi Day is all about this, surely
I repeat to the man who is water-skiing in a bulging

wetsuit and to the woman in a gauzy nightdress
and the man on a bicycle crossing some kind of
finish line with one hand off the handlebars and

a middle finger raised up high.

≠

The healer showed me how to hold the feet
of the dying and bring them the vision
of salt water meeting the fresh

at the estuary
and the shapes this meeting makes.
This was her way of helping her friend let go.

To hold his feet and visualise those whorls –
and it worked. He let go.
Which makes me think about the nineteen-year-old

who wrote to his parents from Gallipoli
all in Māori
promising not to start smoking.

≠

The house feels itself
to be constantly occupied
even when its descendants

are not filling the rooms
with their squabbles and bribes.
The walls remember the chisels

and daughters.
Each new window opened
brings more sounds of breathing

and effort, as if the timber
is finally getting up out of its chair.
Every morning the house

raises its family like a flag.

LOOK AT WHAT WE FUCKING WELL HAVE

Just look at what we fucking well have.
The pocket the packet the postcard the purse
not the hanged man and the constant lightning strike
look at what we have look on it and be grateful.
Look at what we have now the leash the booming
groan all the bright escapology the muddy
line of thrills army of crab apples sea cucumbers.
All this look upon it and be thankful.

Shavings and lather the way the day
waggles like a membrane
such largesse in a straw hat
a spewfarm a spool a Pre-Raphaelite wail
from the saddle lumpish and gone.
A great song of a silken inch fangling into shape
not just the five of pentacles for Christ's sake
the seven of pentacles can't you see the cups and

fucking cups of it where is the gratitude.
The fresh whiff of fish! Angle of yank!
The leaves and the branch for fuck's sake

we have not only the pinch but the golden fucking punch
the doily the strobe the actual fucking original flake
the grain itself the ilk as well as the motherfucking inkling.

All this plus the mild filter the ladle
the bright cicada sound of shrinking
the skim in its entirety all of it do you hear me all of it.

FRIDAY NIGHT

Way down south
in the south
of the south island of himself

an inky moon casts its dark
over greyscale trees.
Eagles and meteorites are not.

Pedestrians, rather,
reflected in spectacles.
No not even

a woman with a blank face
holding a basket of yams.
Misunderstanding the verb

she offers to edit my cup of tea.
In the mirror endless men
slice grilled meat from rotating skewers.

Cardamom pods, ginger powder,
nutmeg, the table steadies us
but where the teapot should be

that black moon again:
it's at his wrists
in the palm of his right hand

punched through the walls of
the apartment
with soaring ceilings.

Blackcircle in boychest.
Blackcircle on girlmouth.
Blackcircle corsage.

KNEE, THROAT

This rigging from which our _____
is swinging, the print of a palm stinging
under so many petals, which are actually kisses.

In the distance a smear of penguin
or land, I look out and it looks back.
I sail onto your drydock, filmed

as if I am scenic. Someone is really hitting
those bells in the clapped out spy-station
so this also sounds like a shipyard

it's not just a metaphor.
How many times can a stranger say *fuck*
aggressively to another stranger for the duration

of an escalator ride? We are about
to find out. His eyes are misty, his face an inflammation.
The steamship lowers its funnel

when it travels under the drooping bridge.
There is a man inside a rubbish bin on Warschauer Strasse
playing it from the inside like a stinking drum.

FILLING IN THE GRAVE

Now the grandsons have a job they can do.
Are they paint or shadow?
There is something of the swan about them.
Are there birds on the horizon?
Clouds of black rise from their shovels,

perhaps believers, or sandflies
or grains of sand. Clouds of
alphabet, impossibly sad faces and someone
struggling up out of them with a guitar.

Perhaps this is Christ himself.
There are black crowds and white crowds.
A man with his ear pressed to a cold mirror.
Are those squalls, or a cling
of tiny black mussels on rock
sharp little barnacles?

In the sky there are muscular men holding each other
or they are holding a baby
or they are holding each other as they would a baby.

They walk and wheel away.
New ones take their place, dust devils,
the earth is sand here.
An older couple like Roman numerals
in Volkswagen-green cardigans.

Spilled cream or cordial a day later.
This is the face of an old man held in his own hands.
The floor is so cold it could be old cocoa.
This is a naked man trying to bend
a naked man trying to get up from bending.
This is people gathered, beast-like,
their bent heads have leaves for ears.

HE KANOHI KITEA

He kanohi kitea, he hokinga mahara
A face seen, a memory stirred

We are high contrast for the camera
black plaits down the fronts of our white shirts.
Behind us a door aches shut.
Beside us gold buttons, Wi Parata's beard
the white bulbs

of the girls' dresses.
All is light, all is light removed.
The pounamu shine of the blade
and the sports team's shins, their shield.
The bright of the white-blue

behind Tamihana's head.
The heavy mere singing its
shape, singing the stone's skim,
the urge of birds.
You women, your tassels.

The weave is golden
and always at our throats
are collars, the moon. Pull my chin
towards you from your height.
Stroke my eyebrow with

the pad of your thumb and say
the word *perpetual,* the word *kneel.*
We are warm in your cloaks.
Unaiki, your skin's glow.
Huria, the listing ship behind you.

PINOCCHIO REX

On receiving good news the graves
opened up and cried and all the black-and-white photographs
poked tissues under their sunglasses.

The wharenui burst into flames for the manuhiri
to light their smokes. Breezeblock Ladies' Toilets glowed pink
in the travel agent sunset.

≠

Matter: in this case, food additives
and their bewitching numbers.
All over the neighbourhood the sentiment

towards you feels just right,
dairy-painted and sandwich-boarded.
This aisle speaks in hymns and lino squeaks, full of

flowers and humming freezers and
that garage-mounted security system
kind of feeling.

≠

Look up, look higher. See that stick figure
holding another stick figure under the water
in celebration, in sponsorship.

Ducks pass and also pūkeko
on their way to mourn at the white line
on a cellular level, magnificent and leathered.

Trains do not run on time, here.
Trains run on tracks, you really do
say that out loud.

THE FANTASY OF BRINGING AN
EXTINCT SPECIES BACK TO LIFE

is no longer sci-fi. Don't turn your back on it.
There are those whose dedication to death and desiccation
is set loose in the water.
Small and long-tailed, blue-black and heavy-clawed, yes

there are those whose dedication to death and desiccation
is nesting again, fidgeting, eating insects.
Small and long-tailed, blue-black and heavy-clawed,
actively competing to carry The Name.

Is nesting, fidgeting, eating insects
such a sin? What say we?
Actively competing to carry the name
Forest-Dweller?

Is it such a sin? What say we?
I for one am a big fan of the Enlightenment.
Forest-Dweller
when the forest was green and every drop sweet.

I for one am a big fan of The Enlightenment.
Not this river of shit pretending to be a bridge.
When the forest was green and every drop sweet
the green was vertical and deserved children.

Not this river of shit pretending to be a bridge
pretending to be a straight-backed gentleman.
The green was vertical and deserved children
and red-collared strumming, teal feathers.

A straight-backed gentleman must
set an alarm plan an outfit find a recipe heat up cool down.
Red-collared strumming, teal feathers
a winking gendarme and a re-roofed revolution:

set an alarm plan an outfit find a recipe heat up cool down.
It is set loose in the water.
A winking gendarme and a re-roofed revolution
is no longer sci-fi. Don't turn your back on it.

THE NIGHT WE FINALLY KILLED HIM

I'll not forget the way his head fell soft to the left
as if his thick neck with its tendons like pylon cables
and three days of sprouting orange stubble
had been instead the slight and feathered
neck of a duck and we'd simply wrung it.

Which we hadn't. It was poison.
And not just a handful of random fizz from a box of
rat poison or some guy-in-a-nightgown's tired lover's
finger-grubby flimsy-mirrored rattling bathroom cabinet.
We weren't that green.

This would leave no trace – well, almost none.
A negligible percentage in his already thickening blood.
I took a picture in my mind, the way you do
when you forget to bring your camera to the zoo.
The room elliptical and red. That chess piece white and blue.

ALMANAC

i

On the sunny street I pass someone selling calendars.
She has the expression of a woman in the rain.
Would you like a calendar, sir?
I stop and turn to her, taking one from her hand.
What is the firefighter's best friend? I ask.
Rain, says the vendor and I pass her my money.

ii

The year runs ahead of me like a train track.
Beside the track is a coastline, the sea is an island.
Orange flowers grow from the retaining wall.
Inside me the presentation and orientation of my organs
is roughly the same as it was seven calendar years ago.
The water, like the lahar, is moving away from me.

iii

When the violinist plays Lilburn, the slow
voice of it becomes two characters in conversation.
Myself and the salesperson and the turbine of our transaction.
Whatever you want to say about the future
says the violin
it's not the report card we thought it would be.

iv

I put the palm of my hand on the pain.
I put the palm of my hand on the number.
The women are leaving, off to be tattooed.
We stay behind and throw nets over meaning, drop ladders
for the dead and the ones they ride in on.
Read the steam from the underground ovens.

I HAVE NO RETIREMENT PLAN

but I have a new vacuum cleaner.
It's a Dirt Devil. I feel so ashamed but
I stagger on, hero on the boil
shoe without a heel, house without ribs.

When I think of the next fifteen years
it's almost as if I were thinking about the next
fifteen dust bunnies: flat as a lambskin
a stoat-grey snow.

But also proud! Proud as a pencil!
This purchase works! Look at us moving
together like wheels, pedalling it all
into memory, into money!

It's almost as if I were thinking.
Hero with a Dirt Devil.
I feel so on the boil.

TONGUE

Wet, red flag on the back
of the diesel ute.
Hanging loose

sweating drool
into his water bowl.
A glinting river:

dog tongue licking
the baked dust
of ducks off stones.

He licks his anus
with that same
strong, tasting muscle

but hygiene
is for cat-lovers.
Dog paw holds down

my right wrist.
Dog breath
a warm stink.

Dog tongue
a hot fish I catch
between fingers.

THE TYPICAL LIGHTNING BOLT

and the same could be said
for all surprises
is less of an emergency than it appears
a spoon standing straight up in sugar flashing
when you flick that big soft kitchen switch

a cake made of its own candle smoke
it disappoints you to death
fumbling with its gun
after burning a finger
filling the hot-water bottle

so let me give you one piece of advice
from one stretch of electrons to another
sing some kind of song when it's maintenance time
and you're walking outside working hours
through the blue canyon of the empty swimming pool

HOW TO SURVIVE ON A PLINTH

I asked a number of horses and hanged dictators
of history and some of the big-name gods
and goddesses, the dog who waited on that train platform,
a statue even then among the commuters.

When all I could find were fountains
I asked the thing with the tail and lifelike scales
glinting in the water's fall and the small children
emptying that same water from pots and urns

and seashells and their own bladders
for centuries into the seasonal air.
I asked the woman at the top of the composition
who named the whole place

and the one whose dress is a lace of language
and the rugby team, the graveyard angels and
their loyal pigeons, silent lions.
I asked a gryphon, a huntaway, a bear,

the man squinting his open eye into his camera
and the other man who walked accidentally into shot.
The soldiers with quiet bayonets
pointing at their acres of paving.

FUNKHAUS

You and I hang limp behind the real thinkers.
We order more moisture into the air we breathe.
We shovel up this morning and sprinkle its grit

(choose our words carefully):
blood? litter? bladder?
We float above our glorious proportions.
Your Berlin sends roots

down through its dead.
Its buildings and its total recall shake with trains.
Words are gold bricks of light in the season.
I drift behind my own thoughts

a street pigeon,
an Egyptian Queen, a Television Tower.
Even my close friends join in.
In the event of fire we are encouraged to shout fire.

You perch on a branch, utterly visible.
What is the word for *suddenly*?

Trucks and their wind gusts lift the leaf litter.
I hope to see a monolith and feel the ground shake.
I hope to open a bank account and send packages

into autumn and winter. But air, water, fire:
and when these elements leave the body?
Tomorrow and September.
You lift at the corners as I pass by.

ONE HIT IS NOT ENOUGH

The Polaroid grows branches, colours and
cousins, rivers, mountains twist and pose
on the high-stepping stiletto
red carpet. We all feel the sting of rain

and justice ha ha ha; we fall in love with hip
hop and out of love with pipelines.
We know we must not forget the password,
the carver father, the eighties, the skylines.

We're carved into sky, born into museums.
People like to see themselves so
they come back and back to the museum
to spear and hand sew in real time.

Marched into land, old money.
Summer holidays are long and memories
centuries, too ha ha ha.
The mana of our wāhine, the wehi, the wana.

Our sashes, they say, are too bright blue,
and one hit's not enough, and neither is two.
We are layers and layers and everywhere, all.
Tapa, tatau, taaniko, demons.

Don't ask me to speak for the nations, we shift
the hate with the light from our fascinators.
We took ourselves out, really far fuckin out
and we took passengers, too

from the Kitchen of Miracles to the wānangananga.
Document this, and document this motherfucker:
the graduate, the groove, the rangatiratanga.
Break that fantasy, please wake you all up.

We're eating the beast, it frees us to surf.
Chop up the hui and swallow the suey
and origin, listen, sizzle and muscle, story and school us
and shark us and weapon and curse.

NOTES

MOTHER was first published in tribute to Tapu Te Ranga marae following the fire in 2019. It appeared on the blog for the Te Hā Māori writers conference 2019 (kaituhimaori.org.nz/2019/08/27/ mother-by-hinemoa-baker/). The line that begins 'Whakataka te hau . . .' is lifted from a well-known waiata/karakia which, according to www.folksong.org.nz, was first published in *Maori Mementos* by Charles Davis in 1855.

IF I HAD TO SING was commissioned on the 2015 re-opening of Christchurch Art Gallery Te Puna o Waiwhetū after the devastating earthquakes of 2010–11. It was also published in *Solid Air: Australian and New Zealand Spoken Word*, edited by David Stavanger and Anne-Marie Te Whiu (University of Queensland Press, 2019). The video version is at christchurchartgallery.org.nz/multimedia/ audiotour/hinemoana-baker. The poem owes the image of cities which 'still live in my mirrors' to Italo Calvino.

AUNTIES borrows its concept and canter from part one of Joy Harjo's 'She Had Some Horses'. An audio version was first published on Paula Green's blog *NZ Poetry Shelf*: nzpoetryshelf.com/2019/04/11/ poetry-shelf-audio-spot-hinemona-baker-reads-aunties/

NARCISSIST ADVICE COLUMN was first published in *Poetry* (July/ August 2016): poetryfoundation.org/poetrymagazine/poems/89748/ narcissist-advice-column

DECEMBER, FLOHMARKT and TONGUE were first published as poetry posters by Phantom Billstickers.

THE TYPICAL LIGHTNING BOLT was first published somewhere I'm sure but for the life of me I can't remember where. My apologies!

HOW TO SURVIVE ON A PLINTH and KNEE, THROAT were first published by *4th Floor Literary Journal* 2019: 4thfloorjournal. co.nz/hinemoana-baker/

WAIATA TANGI features an epigraph from the poem 'Sunrise' by Robert Hass, from *Praise* (first published by Ecco Press, 1979, New York, NY).

WAITANGI DAY features a line from PJ Harvey's song 'The Letter': 'Who is left that writes these days?'

LOOK AT WHAT WE FUCKING WELL HAVE was written in support of the occupation at Ihumātao, and was first published in *Te Rito o te Harakeke – A collection of writing for Ihumātao*, produced by Rangatahi o te Pene, Hana Pera Aoake, Sinead Overbye, Michelle Rahurahu Scott and essa may ranapiri. You can watch the video version here: vimeo.com/351183294

FILLING IN THE GRAVE was first published in the New Zealand edition of *Best American Poetry 2014*, edited by Gregory O'Brien: blog.bestamericanpoetry.com/the_best_american_poetry/2014/07/ poetry-from-aotearoanew-zealand-4-hinemoana-bakers-burial. html

HE KANOHI KITEA features a traditional kīwaha as its epigraph.

ALMANAC was first published as 'Calendar' by Richard Nash in *Sirens*, March 2014, and pays homage in part to Giacomo Leopardi.

NGĀ MIHI MUTUNGA KORE

Mum, Teresia, Tiahuia. Moe mai rā koutou ngā wāhine rangatira, wāhine māia. Moe mai, takoto mai rā i roto i te rangimārie. Ki ōku tīpuna me āku whānau nō Te Āti Awa, nō Raukawa ki te Tonga, nō Ngāi Tahu, nō Ngāti Kiritea – tēnā koutou. Aroha nui to my dad, Val – thank you for your love of me and of the sea – and to Aunty Pauline, Linda and Louise.

Ehara taku toa i te toa takitahi, engari he toa takitini.

So many friends and whānau have loved me through life over the last five hard years, and some of you have also published me, invited me to festivals or gigs, filmed or recorded me, given me guitars, pointed me towards other writings I have loved, read my manuscripts, reviewed my poems, translated my work and/or all of the above. Tusiata Avia, Marty Smith, Kate Camp, Maria McMillan, Stefanie Lash, Sarah Jane Barnett, Emelihter Kihleng, Leonardo Carta, Francesca Benocci, Marian Witham and whānau, Lynn Davidson, Helen Heath, Morgan Gwynneth Bach, Joan Fleming, Charles Olsen, Naomi Arnold, Sarah Wilson, Maryja Martysievič, Sarah Yolanda Castaño, Regina Dyck, Craig Santos Perez, Silke Hilgers, Mara Mahía, Marten and Gabriele Hahn, Felix and the Wassermann whānau, Bridget van der Zijpp, Karl Dunn, Iain and Marian Fraser, Matthias Kniep, Nadja Küchenmeister, Ulrike Almut Sandig, Sebastian Reuter, Enana Asr, Danny Al Haoui, Mohamad Halbouni, Ulrike Brauns, Laura Naumann and Henrike Iglesias, Tania Wehrs, Jörg Keveloh, Paula Green, Madeleine Slavick, Gaye Sutton, Stef Lauer, William Connor, Steffen Kreft, Moon, Sofia, Marit and Marie, the Schokoladen whānau, Angela Boyd, Christine White, Jim and Kelly and the Phantom Billstickers whānau – all of my love to you beautiful, generous folks. Special thanks to Victor Rodger, for giving me Ben Lerner's book and for your continued tautoko of our young writers. Aroha always to Bill Manhire, to Fergus Barrowman, Ashleigh Young and all the team at Victoria University Press and to Viggo Mortensen and all at Perceval Press.

Tusiata – thank you my heart. Your alofa and wisdoms keep me afloat. Always holding you and Sepela close. Anahera Gildea – kāore he kupu, my whanaunga. Tū tonu mai, e te māreikura. You can't know what you have meant to me, my wairua, my writing, and of course to my boxes that are still under your garage. Hans Kellett, I love you(nicorn). Thank you for giving me a heartfelt hug of a home here in Berlin. Kia ora to you too, Andreas Waldbaum and Abdul Alzuabi – may we share many more small pastries and big conversations at our kitchen table.

Many of these poems were written during my time as Victoria University Writer in Residence 2014, as Creative New Zealand Berlin Writer in Residence 2016, as well as during a short residency in 2017 at Ebenböckhaus in Munich. Without this support this book would not have been possible.

Photographs by (and a big mihi to) Ashley Clark. Appreciation is due to Judith Geare and all at the Goethe-Institut in Wellington for your support of my journey and language-learning in Berlin. My gratitude again to everyone who contributed to my 2015 Boosted crowd-funding campaign – thank you for supporting me and my writing. I am humbled and grateful, always.

Lastly, big love to those friends who take me for the best walks, leave hair on my clothes and lick my face: Tai, Moss, Lucy, Elvis, Pepe, Poppy, Leo, Butterbean, Ramona, Jed, Meg, Kyah, Eddie, Bille, Trixie, Begemot and Tui.

Woof.

x

Hinemoana